KT-212-875

Moral Panic

Moral Panic

Exposing the religious right's agenda on sexuality

Theresa Murray with
Michael McClure

CASSELL

Other titles in the Listen Up! series
in the Cassell Sexual Politics list include

With Friends Like These...

Marxism and gay politics

Simon Edge

State Of The Queer Nation

A critique of gay and lesbian politics

in 1990s Britain

Chris Woods

Lesbophobia!

Gay men and misogyny

Megan Radclyffe

We Don't Want to March Straight!

Masculinity, queers and the military

Peter Tatchell

Fighting Words

An open letter to queers and radicals

Scott Tucker

For a catalogue of related titles in our Sexual Politics/Global Issues list please write to us at the address below:

Cassell plc
Wellington House
125 Strand
London
WC2R 0BB

215 Park Avenue South
New York
NY 10003

We are grateful to John McDade, editor of *The Month*, for permission to reproduce here portions of Michael McClure's article published in that journal.

© 1995 Theresa Murray and Michael McClure

All rights reserved. No part of this publication may be reproduced or transmitted in any form or by any means, electronic or mechanical including photocopying, recording or any information storage or retrieval system, without prior permission in writing from the publishers.

First published 1995

British Library Cataloguing-in-Publication Data
A catalogue record for this book is available from the British Library.

ISBN: 0-304-33327-1

Design and typesetting by
Ben Cracknell

Printed and bound in Great Britain by
Biddles Ltd, Guildford and King's Lynn

Contents

Introduction 1

Lethal Discourse 5

The Impotence of Being Earnest 17

The Perpetuation of Control 23

Special Interests? 28

A Time of Change 31

Ambiguous Places 34

Generalities and Myths 37

Alternatives 40

Back to Basics? 44

What's in a 'Nature'? 50

An Unnecessary Problem 55

Notes 57

Hear the word of the Lord,
you who tremble at his word:
"Your brethren who hate you
and cast you out for my name's sake
have said, 'Let the Lord be
glorified, and that we may see your joy';
but it is they who shall be put
to shame."

Isaiah 66:5

About the Authors

Terri Murray is an American feminist writer and activist. She holds a bachelor of fine arts in film and television from New York University, where she also did post graduate work in religious studies. She also holds a bachelor of arts in philosophy and theology from Heythrop College, University of London.

Michael McClure works within the Roman Catholic tradition of ministry as a secular priest of the Archdiocese of Westminster, London. He has six years experience in pastoral ministry and is presently studying for a master of theology at Heythrop College, University of London.

We would like to add thanks to Rebecca Davies for providing invaluable technical support.

Introduction

Ideas can be dangerous things. Their potential for destruction and distortion is as boundless as their creative force. Very often our knee-jerk reactions are responses to our beliefs *about* things and have little or nothing to do with the things themselves. A friend who was staying in Africa once reacted with horror to the sight of a big hairy spider on the wall of his room. He believed that the spider was a poisonous tarantula. But when he consulted a native African (my friend was Scottish) the fellow calmly picked up the harmless creature and carried it outside. From the native's perspective my friend's reaction was amusing and exaggerated. But to me his response was quite natural.

The point of this pamphlet is not simply to demonstrate that people can have different perspectives on the same thing, while neither need be right or wrong. Lesbians, gay men, feminists and other advocates of multiculturalism have often been accused of *relativism* by the pundits of the Christian right. We, in turn, have often accused them of the same thing, except that they choose to describe their own agenda as 'God's', hence incurring an *additional* charge of moral conceit. Knowing that this declaration stands in need of some authority besides their own testimony, they appeal to the Bible to justify their claim that God is on their side. But this is hardly an independent court of appeal, since the Bible is a set of ancient writings which have been hand-picked by Fathers of the Church who had a vested interest in tailoring the selection to fit *their* agenda. But even the orthodox interpretation of the *existing* cannon was by no means uncontroversial. On the contrary, it is the product of a long process of eliminating and anathematizing alternative views. Even despite their internal contradictions, the sixty six books of the Bible have a fairly homogenous outlook on women and on the hierarchical social structure, which is no more than a reflection of the pecking order that was typical of its Greco-Roman milieu.

What in fact makes particular religious hypotheses 'true' is the power that men have had to persuade people to hold them. That men (and often their adoring wives) still do have this power is attested by a recent report in the *Guardian* which said that one in four Americans now describe themselves as evangelical Christians.

Some who take this line may advert to the democratic process, claiming that the ideological battle was won by popular consensus – fair and square – so what on earth is wrong with that? We would say that nothing on earth is wrong with that, but our opponents are not content to claim that anything on *earth* is 'right' with their position – its 'rightness' comes from God above!

Our point in mentioning my friend's reaction to his belief about big hairy spiders was simply to show that beliefs about things do not always correspond to the facts of the matter. Truth ought to be what gives a public belief system its legitimacy, not vice versa. Is the Christian belief system the only legitimate one? And is there really only one Christian belief system? The Pope dictates moral prescriptions to Catholic Christians worldwide, but is looked upon by many Protestant Christians as the Anti-Christ. Christianity stands alongside other monotheistic belief systems which make equally radical claims about the truth of their texts and their prophets. Who is right? Whose belief is true?

In this pamphlet we sketch briefly two theories of truth: the realist (or correspondence) theory and the anti-realist (or coherence) theory. In the correspondence theory, truth is some kind of a relation between facts or reality, on the one hand, and beliefs, statements, etc on the other. 'Truth', in this theory, is conformity with fact; agreement with reality. Meanwhile, proponents of the coherence theory of truth argue that those propositions are true which cohere with the largest organized system of consistent propositions. If we rely on coherence as a test of truth, we can canonize any statement we choose so long as it fits into our network of mutually consistent statements.

Since the religious right's rhetoric suggests that they hold a realist view of truth (ie non-relativistic), a large part of this pamphlet is devoted to showing that their methodology is inappropriate to this view. Though our argument is polemical, we are not on a mission to destroy anyone's faith. We are not nihilists. We, like our opponents, are Christians. Having said that, we would be a lot more modest about claiming to have earned that title, since we view Christianity as the imitation of Christ. The version of Christianity which we outline in this pamphlet is one which we feel may appeal to anyone (regardless of sex or sexual orientation) who views Christian discipleship chiefly as a commitment to a relationship with God.

Moral Panic

one

Lethal Discourse

According to the *Oxford Modern English Dictionary*, an 'apologetic' is 'a reasoned defence, especially of Christianity'. In undertaking a gay and lesbian apology, then, we are taking for granted several presuppositions. First, we maintain that our view is an essentially 'Christian' one. Second, we are aware that there are an increasing number of self-proclaimed 'Christians' who deny that the word 'Christian' is conceivably applicable to our cause, or to any cause other than those traditionally or historically espoused by 'Christian' social institutions. Third, we are taking for granted the propriety of rational argument as our method, although we hope to call attention to the limits of such an argument. If one cannot defend faith on rational grounds, then this carries certain consequences which we are prepared to accept.

Nearly all of these premises are controversial and they are internally related to one another in ways which we shall attempt to explicate. Our first premise concerns the meaning of a word or the content given to it. This is a crucial point. Fifty years ago, people either said, 'I believe that Jesus Christ is my Lord and Saviour' or they did not. Those who did were 'Christians' and those who did not were pagans, or members of another faith. Nowadays, however, theology recognizes that things aren't so simple. Words depend for their meaning upon the frame of reference within which they are used. To use moral language is to adopt a particular intersubjective perspective, in the case of 'Christianity' this means viewing reality through the lenses of a value-laden hypothesis. Within particular forms of life, words are conventional, that is, they serve a function which is agreed to be desirable or important (ie meaningful) from the point of view of those who use them. We see how words go out of currency and come into it as the frame of reference (form of life) evolves. For example, modern talk of 'software' or 'information superhighways' or 'homophobia' or being 'in the closet' would have had no meaning or completely different ones ten or twenty years ago.

The content or meaning of such terms is directly related to their purpose or function. In this sense words are mechanisms much like other public tools. Take, for example, a traffic light. Its purpose is to help pedestrians cross streets safely. It would hardly make sense to stop and wait at an intersection simply because the signal is red if it were 4 am and there were no traffic coming in either direction for miles. If our docile pedestrian were to obey the signal under these circumstances he would have ceased to use it as a means to a desirable end and would have come to regard it as an end in itself. Instead of the convention working *for* him, it would work *instead of* him, such that his own reasoning faculty or prerogative becomes obsolete. Likewise, if our methods of transportation evolved so that automobiles were no longer in use, then it would be ridiculous to obey the traffic lights just out of nostalgia for the old tradition.

Our point is that the meaning given to words is context-relative. To take another example, if a priest holds up a wafer and says 'This is the body of Christ' it does no good for a scientist to snatch up the wafer, take it to a lab, and perform all sorts of clinical tests to determine whether it has the organic composition of human flesh. If the scientist denies, from her frame of reference, that the so-called 'body of Christ' is the body of anyone, she is wrong, according to the priest, not because her experiments were faulty but because she didn't understand what he meant in saying the words 'this is the body of Christ'. For the scientist, the application of the word 'body' in that context seems bizarre indeed. Whereas, for the priest it is 'natural' (ie normative). Another good example of this conflict between differing frames of reference appears in the film, *The God's Must Be Crazy*. A Kalahari Bushman, in need of sustenance, innocently shoots a gazelle with a poisonous arrow. From his perspective, animals are not anyone's personal 'property' (the whole idea of 'personal property' is alien to the Bushman, who has accidentally wandered into 'civilization' for the first time in his life). The Bushman is shot in the leg by the 'landowner' who sees the Bushman's act as 'poaching'. In this example, as in the previous one, the description of certain acts or objects depends upon the form of life from which they derive their meaning (ie they are 'context relative'). We shall return to this point later. For now the important issue is meaning, not truth. We can use words successfully (meaningfully) without knowing anything at all about the truth or even the existence of that to which they refer. We spend thousands of dollars on 'the cure for cancer' and yet we do not really know whether such a thing exists. We are not speaking nonsense when we talk about 'the first woman president', even if such a thing has never been instantiated and even if it never will be. These words get their meaning from hypothetical modes of thought, not from an independent reality. What is important within the system, is that they 'work' or are meaningful to those who use them.

Our second premise concerns the presupposition of our opponents that we are not entitled to a different frame of reference with respect to the use of the word 'Christianity', but must, if we are to use it *truthfully* adopt *theirs*. Thus, the *true* meaning of the word can only be found within the context in which it makes sense to them. The main point here is that we are *defending* our perspective (or our right to have one). This however has not been the picture which has emerged from conservative 'Christian' groups and spokespersons, who label homosexuals who seek to enter into rational dialogue with the traditional forces 'aggressive'. This is clear, for instance, in the public statement issued by the Ramsey Colloquium (a group of twenty one eminent theologians and academics in the US) whose members described the social phenomenon of the homosexual movement as 'a gay and lesbian movement that aggressively proposes radical changes in social behaviour, religion, morality and law'.[1] They go on to allege that, 'what is confusedly at work here is an extreme individualism, a claim for autonomy so extreme that it *must* undercut the common good'. [my emphasis] Likewise, the Church of England accuses lesbians and gay men of 'taking up a defiant stance, demonstrating their pride in being gay or lesbian, and making exaggerated claims and demands'.[2] Last but not least, Pope John Paul II in his recent Papal encyclical *Veritatis Splendor* insists that the process of questioning the Roman Catholic Church's moral teaching 'is no longer a matter of limited and occasional dissent, but of an overall systematic calling into question of traditional moral doctrine on the basis of certain anthropological and ethical presuppositions'.[3]

All of these statements display a flat refusal to acknowledge *their own* presuppositions and the effects of those presuppositions on others who are made to live like aliens within 'the only' normative social context (or frame of reference). In our experience, when we are accused of 'radical' and 'extreme' behaviour, this typically refers to *anything other than* total secrecy coupled with a large dose of self-denigration...in other words, behaviour which, when applied to heterosexual males, is 'normal'. It follows from this that a double standard is 'normal', which we have never doubted. The question is whether it *ought* to remain so. What these accusors fail to recognize is that what they call 'aggression' is only identified as such against the backdrop of an ideology so totalitarian as to be beyond reflective self-analysis. The epithets ascribed to homosexuals (such as 'abnormality', 'perversity', 'pathology' and 'failure') by the self-appointed 'moral authorities' all depend on an unquestioned hetero-male reality in comparison to which all else is deemed inferior or only 'relatively' good.

The irony of the situation is not only that those who actually inflict suffering and systematic exclusion refuse to acknowledge or feel remorse for doing so, but that, in addition, they deploy what one commentator dubbed 'the counter-victim flip', whereby the offender quickly jumps on the defensive. Before any serious blame can be cast on the the victimizer he has miraculously been transformed into the victim. We see this form of evasive irresponsibility on a much broader scale than on lesbian and gay issues.

One of Newt Gingrich's least discussed accomplishments as House Speaker was his remedial skill in changing the Enola Gay exhibit at the Smithsonian Institution to accord with his pro-American view of history. Gingrich, appalled at a taxpayer-funded display that condemned the dropping of an atomic bomb on Hiroshima in 1945 and sympathized with the Japanese, negotiated an alternative with Smithsonian Secretary I Michael Heyman. Now only the Enola Gay, the plane that dropped the bomb, is on display. When queried as to his objections, Gingrich replied, 'You mean other than the fact that it was historically inaccurate, anti-American, and distorted history?' There are ominous similarities between his tactics and the propaganda strategies employed by Goebbels which won popular support for anti-Semitism. Jay W Baird, in his book, *The Mythical World of Nazi War Propaganda, 1939-1945* writes:

> The peculiar genius of Hitler and Goebbels was to merge the themes of traditional German patriotism with Nazi ideological motifs, a course pursued from the days of the earliest Munich rallies in 1919 until 1945. … By uniting patriotism and Nazi ideology Hitler forged a compelling weapon against what he called 'the immorality of Weimar rationalism', the symbol of cultural decadence, racial impurity, and Jewish putrefaction.[4]

Gingrich commented further that the original Enola Gay exhibit reflected, 'the enormous underlying pressure in the elite intellegensia to be anti-American, to despise American culture, to rewrite history and to espouse a set of values which are essentially destructive'.[5]

A similar phemenon has occured with Affirmative Action, the US program that seeks to give African Americans and other underprivileged groups preferential treatment in jobs, education, and public contracts (presumably because the government acknowledges the debt it owes to them and wants to atone for its own arbitrary privilege). The program is now nefariously referred to as 'reverse racism'. The use of the word 'racism' in this application evokes the same negative associations which made the word meaningful in the civil rights movement of the 1960s, but now it is deployed to the advantage of those who already have the advantage, as opposed to those who don't. Again, this is a way of re-describing things to suit the self-image of the 'victimized' and ever-innocent patriarch.

Another example which always seems to be obvious to everyone but Americans is the portrait painted in textbooks and Hollywood movies of the white settlers of North America as if they were 'cowboy heros'. In March 1995 Sioux Indians in South Dakota were in bitter dispute with federal authorities over plans to turn the site of the Battle of Wounded Knee into a National Park, with a visitor's centre featuring audio-visual exhibits. The Sioux are concerned that the exhibits will downplay the slaughter. They recall when the National Park Service opened the Custer Battle site. He was made into a hero and it took them years to get the name changed.

The main point of our second premise is to assert that we, and *not* our opponents, are on the defensive. What we want is not revenge, but to redress the balance. Our concern is not to start something new but to end something old, namely, systematic oppression.

The Catholic writer Charles Taylor takes the defensive tone in the following statement from his book, *Multiculturalism and the Politics of Recognition*:

> … the further demand that we are looking at here is that we all *recognize* the equal value of different cultures; that we not only let them survive, but acknowledge their worth.[6]

What makes this (hopefully) naive statement so funny is that lesbians and gay men live with what Taylor ominously calls this 'further demand' on them every day. A description of homosexual experience which could paraphrase his statement might go as follows:

... the further demand we are looking at every day of our lives is that we all recognize the superior value of the dominant culture; that we not only tolerate it but that we aquiesce in it without resistance.

The possibility which Taylor seems to dread is an *actuality* for countless gay and lesbian individuals, may they not dread it? According to the Church of England's report, *Issues in Human Sexuality* [para.4.17, p.37] all people, men and women, '*should* come to understand and to *value* [heterosexual] complimentarity'. [my emphasis] This document is rich with masculine and feminine stereotyping, even claiming that 'a man looks at spiritual truths differently from a woman'. Likewise the members of the Ramsey Colloquium describe marriage as 'the normative vision *required* for social well being'. [p.263, my emphasis]

The third and last of our presuppositions is probably the most controversial and it is related to the first. What role (if any) should reason play in the validation (or invalidation) of religious belief-systems? Does one have to provide empirical evidence to prove that a particular belief system is true? Must it even be *possible* to prove that a belief-system is true? To say that a statement is true is to say that it can be verified according to some relevant test, or criterion. Hence, the criteria used to 'test the truth' are agreed upon by concensus within a particular community. This view of truth is an anti-realist one, and we do not claim that it is the only possible or correct view of truth. In this concept of truth, if the majority of people in a particular culture agreed on the truth of propositions such as 'mutilating young girls is good' or 'kicking the elderly is right', then we could all be certain that this truth was beyond reproach. Absolute truth however is not necessarily the same thing as absolute concensus or assent.

Let us assume that faith is a *risk-taking* decision which goes beyond what can be proved or rationally guaranteed. If one describes religious belief in this way then she belongs to a school known as *realism*. The religious realist claims that language about God is true if it refers or corresponds to a God who exists independently of the universe

He has created. On this view truth is 'verification transcendent'. This means that whether a statement is true or false is not dependent upon the tests which we think are appropriate, but that their ultimate truth depends upon whether they correspond to some ultimate reality independent of our tests. Our first presupposition (above) dealt with what it *means* to say 'God exists' or 'Jesus Christ is my Lord and Saviour'. Here we are dealing with the issue of truth. What makes certain theistic utterances true? The realist maintains that the truth of a statement and the verification of a statement are separate issues. Just as in science 'the way things are' may be independent of our best theories and hypotheses, so religion may be attempting a similar exercise.[7]

The realist view, however, poses difficulties for public concensus, since the realist view of truth is not tantamount to knowledge, and all of our knowledge is context-relative. Truth, for the realist, is not dependent upon the meaning given to it within a particular form of life, but is an independent standard which human beings search for in a critical way. A J Ayer writes:

> The statement that what is known must be true is ambiguous. It may mean that it is necessary that if something is known it is true; or it may mean that if something is known it is a necessary truth. The first of these propositions is correct; it re-states the linguistic fact that what is not true cannot properly be said to be known. But the second is in general false. It would follow from the first only if all truths were necessary, which is not the case.[8]

The anti-realist, on the other hand, tends towards the view that 'truths aren't discovered, they're made'. In the anti-realist's view, theological truths are a product of the form of life in which they make sense. They are context-relative. As people of faith we are concerned, as perhaps many of our opponents are, to preserve a realist concept of truth in Christianity. We believe that there is an ultimate Truth of the matter for all religious or moral statements, although we may not *know* what it is. As we said, this approach to faith is one which we feel involves risk-taking – a commitment to an uncertainty. The question is *who runs the realist's risk*? We hold a realist view commonly known as *fideism* (the word is derived from the Latin word *fides*, meaning 'faith').

On this view the most fundamental assumptions are derived from religious faith *itself*. Religious faith itself is the foundation of one's life. The fideist's beliefs are 'fundamental' in the sense that they provide the basic, overarching guidance for the way he lives his life; they establish his direction, his goals and his reason for living.[9] But it does not follow from this that these beliefs are 'fundamental' in the sense of being *more obviously true* than anything else he knows or believes, say, from everyday experience or perception. There may be other truths which are 'fundamental' *in our knowledge* (ie epistemologically fundamental) though they by no means provide the sort of 'fundamental guidance' for our living that is offered by religious beliefs.

The fideist will hold that to subordinate faith to reason on questions concerning how he ought to direct his life, his behaviour, etc is a mistake. For some people the idea that religious faith may be freely accepted without reference to any proof or verification tests seems preposterous, but we want to say that it is possible to trust in God without these external supports. The Danish thinker Soren Kierkegaard (1813–55) felt that it was as trivial to choose to believe in God on the basis of detatched objective arguments as it would be to select one's spouse on the basis of points scored in a beauty or bodybuilding contest.[10] Kierkegaard says:

> Without risk there is no faith. Faith is precisely the contradiction between the infinite passion of the individual's inwardness and the objective uncertainty. If I am capable of grasping God objectively, I do not believe, but precisely because I cannot do this I must believe. If I wish to preserve myself in faith I must constantly be intent upon holding fast the objective uncertainty...[11]

There is an alternative approach to realism which seems to represent the ethos of the Christian right on both sides of the Atlantic. This approach is formally known as 'Reformed Epistemology', though many evangelicals who never heard of the technical phrase subscribe wholeheartedly to the view. Reformed epistemologists maintain that *it is rational* to believe without any justification.[12] The truth of their religious utterances is not arrived at by a process of argument. There are no inferences made to arrive at this conclusion, instead the believer is directly aware of God's presence or of God speaking to him or her through the Bible.

That it is *rational* to believe without any justification, puts a new twist on the word 'rational' indeed. The idea that rationality and justification go hand in hand is surely not one that most 'Christians' would want to dispense with in other areas of their lives, such as science, politics, education, sociology, history, etc. Most Christians would not trust, say, a doctor who just knew directly, from looking at his charts, that we needed to undergo surgery. Surely the doctor would need to justify performing surgery on more rational grounds than direct awareness of his charts. What could justify this variation in the meaning of the word 'rational' across contexts?

We do not object to the categorical uniqueness of faith as an area different from other human disciplines. But we do object to the application of the term 'rational' to beliefs which are not justifiable. If faith will dictate what 'rationality' means, then it cannot do so on rational grounds, or else it is not faith. Reformed epistemology sees no real conflict between reason and faith – reason must simply be subordinated to faith. This approach effectively eliminates the risk factor in faith by by abolishing objective uncertainty on grounds which are not justified.

The obvious counter-argument is that *any* group can claim that they are rationally justified in believing *anything* simply on the ground that they are right and others are wrong. My family and friends may subscribe to a script which was revealed to our ancestor by the angel Marcello, who wrote it down over fifteen centuries ago in an ancient language. We may believe that we receive a special replenishing power when we join hands and sing 'Kumbaya' under the full moon. We may say that those who reject this practice are 'sinners' because they are deficient in the sacred moonglow, which alone can restore them to eternal life.

The main difference between the fideist and the reformed epistemologist is that the first accepts the faith commitment knowing that he could possibly be mistaken, whereas the latter believes because he is certain he is right. In the reformed epistemologist's view, faith is no different from knowledge, except that it does not need to be justified. What we want to say is that the religious realist cannot have his cake and eat it. If he is a realist he must admit that he could be wrong, even if he feels confident that he isn't. Otherwise it is difficult to see how he could answer the charge that his 'faith' just amounts to hijacking the words 'rational' or 'epistemology'.

Martin E Marty and R Scott Appleby, in their comprehensive study of comparative fundamentalism, found that not only is fundamentalism 'very rationalistic' but that "its rationalism counters the more regularly supported post-Enlightenment rationalisms".[13] Marty's observation is crucial to an understanding of the religious right's epistemology. While Protestant fundamentalism tends to be based on revelation, neo-scholastic thought tends to be characterised by a Cartesian naive realism. Naive realism is essentially a 'what you see is what you get' theory of knowledge. Descartes held that a criterion for what is true or possible in the natural world is to be found in the clarity and distinctness of our IDEAS. He felt that it was safe to assume that God in his goodness would not deceive us. Thomas Aquinas, William of Ockham and Descartes all felt pretty confident that they could understand the natures of things. However, they all took for granted their own definitions and beliefs about phenomena, and mistakenly assumed that the terminology they used to refer to things in the world was a *criterion* for determining what was actually the case, rather than merely a logically necessary way of expressing their current beliefs.

We would advocate a more cautious version of realism. Critical realism is essentially a 'what you see is what you get... and you ain't seen nothing yet' theory of knowledge. Knowledge is regarded as a tentative basis for certainty, but is by no means unrevisable or only randomly revisable. How and when we revise our terminology is a matter of evidence and of *truth*.

For the religious realist, the notion that theoretical terms really refer to an independent state of affairs (eg the existence of God, or the reality of sin) cannot be proven solely on the basis of the success of the religious enterprise. Theoretical terms may sometimes refer, but whether they refer to ontologically independent realities cannot be determined by how well the religious community succeeds in eliciting predictable effects from their employment. Even if the entire species were one day evangelized into compliance with a particular theological system, and as a result the planet became one big homogenous, morally infallible society, this could not, on a realist view, establish reference to an ontologically independent moral truth or law. It would simply show that we are very powerful, very persuasive human beings, and that our conventions are very successful in serving the ends which we believe are most useful or important.

What Protestant and Catholic fundamentalisms seem to have in common is a typically Cartesian outlook. In Descartes we find a reduction of Eternal or Divine Truths to epistemology – things cannot be other than they appear because God would not deceive us. Marty ascribes to the Protestant fundamentalist mentality a penchant for Baconian inductivism which might be a bit of an insult to Bacon, who at least had the perspicacity to identify *The Idols of the Marketplace* as one of the hindrances to discovery and learning. R S Woolhouse describes them as follows:

The Idols of the Marketplace are the pernicious influences which words and language can have over us. Our own categories impress us by their familiarity as being natural and correct; we continue to use words which are ill-defined, or are part of a false or outmoded way of thought.[14]

two

The Impotence of Being Earnest

What right wing Christian groups fail to understand is that it is one thing to suffer for your beliefs and another to inflict suffering for them. Jesus had the courage of his convictions and proved it, not by aggressively asserting himself but by accepting the consequences of his freedom, his risk-taking concept of truth. Jesus' earthly ministry was was an exemplary exercise in humility, for he showed that conviction and humility could be united in the same thought. When one is tempted by the thought that one's moral duty is the highest, and that doing it gives one license to cause suffering to others, it is difficult to see how this attitude differs from the Pharisees, who crucified Jesus for offending the 'normative' religious code.

The crucial difference between Jesus and the Pharisees was not the content of their belief (both claimed to be obeying the divine commands of Yahweh) but the form which that belief took. Jesus was willing to suffer all for his relationship to God, while the Pharisees were willing to *do* all for their relationship to God, including commiting a murder which did not involve them personally in the suffering and fate of the victim.

Our objection is that moralists look to Jesus for an objective answer to the question 'What is truth?' In expecting a rational response, they are no different from Pilate, who put the question to Jesus face-to-face. The tragic irony in Pilate's question was that he had to ask it at all in the midst of a man who stood prepared to suffer all for his convictions. Jesus' life, and the willingness which it represented to love and to suffer rather than to inflict harm, stood proxy for the rhetoric of 'truth'. It was the scribes and Pharisees of the Temple who specialized in 'searching the Scriptures' for the truths which would serve as evidence in support of the charges against Jesus. Pilate could not accept silence as the answer to his question, which indicates that he was seeking an objective answer – the type of answer which might be deemed acceptable to philosophy.

Jesus' message (which took the form of a life) was and is an offence to the moral guardians of the very religion which he claimed to represent. There was no intellectual or doctrinal dignity in anything he taught. His acts of love stood as ends in themselves; they had nothing to commend them beyond their appeal to the faith of those who witnessed them.

Humility is an ambiguous concept which can often deceive. One may misconstrue humility as some sort of unrelenting servility to one's own beliefs. To submit to the content of your own beliefs is not humility. On the contrary, it is vain complacency. By 'complacency' we do not mean idle inactivity, but an unquestioning certainty that all of one's activities are 'good' or 'valuable' or indispensable to God's purposes. The irony is that the urgency is fueled by the belief that one's own importance is beyond reproach. Unswerving adherence to your own ideas or identity is *dogmatism*... not humility.

Jesus warns of any reduction of the good which could serve as a speculative basis for worshipping him. In Mark 10.17–18 a man runs up to Jesus and kneels before him, asking him, 'Good teacher, what must I do to inherit eternal life?' Jesus responds, 'Why do you call me good? No one is good but God alone'. Set as it is within a chapter that deals with the incommensurability between human values and the demands of the Kingdom, this saying is quite radical. Intellectual dignity and moral values top the list of earthly 'possessions' which must be left behind for the sake of the Kingdom. Jesus advocates a discipleship based on trust instead.

What, then, can we say about Jesus' conviction? How did his faithfulness differ from other forms of zealous courage? The difference, it seems, is between form and content. What Jesus emphasized was not that his followers understood *what* he understood, but that they understood *how* he understood, or in the same way that he understood. His self-communication took the form of a life. His mesage was conveyed through parable and example – methods which allowed his witnesses to 'see for themselves' (not merely to see what Jesus saw but to see as he saw). Jesus didn't tell people what to do he showed them what to do by doing it himself. This is the difference between an authentic Christian and a theocratic dictator. To the dictator, you submit to a proposition because you know it is true. What he lacks in absolute certainty (which is humanly impossible) he compensates for through self-assertion. To the Christian, you submit to your own ignorance in the belief that God alone knows what is true and good. The difference between (a) submitting to what you know God knows, and (b) submitting to the fact that God knows and you don't, is vast. To commit to **a** will give you license to take a tyrannical attitude towards others because of your beliefs, while a commitment to **b** demands a necessary degree of modesty.

Jesus did not seek to restore the world to God ('my Kingdom is not of this world') but trusted God to *restore him* in a way which exiled him from the world and the respectability bestowed on men by common rationality. Both the 'Back to Basics' campaign in the UK and the 'Family Values' which are canvassed in the US are not primarily interested in religious observance (which we see as a matter of individual choice) but rather are modern political movements which use religion as a basis for their attempt to win or consolidate power and extend social control. The methods which they use (as Marty says, 'they *know* how to use the media') betray their anti-realist loyalties. If Truth were not a matter of consensus, then Gingrich and his ilk would not be so intent upon 'zeroing out' the alternatives. If the hegemony of a set of values is their only aim then that is one thing, but in that case they should have the honesty to admit that absolute 'truth' and 'values' are interchangeable in their vocabulary.

In Britian Christianity is the State religion and still has blasphemy laws on the books. Renewed efforts are being made by the Tory right to promote Christian religious education and worship in state schools. Similarly in the US, there is increasing pressure from the Republican right to enforce prayer in schools and to inculcate the young with stereotypes which eliminate choice in the expression of their sexual identity. 'Christian' groups like Operation Rescue orchestrate attacks on abortion clinics in an attempt to eliminate women's reproductive choice.

Humility is central to the fideist's stance. Because we are realists, we must be prepared to countenance the possibility that our opponents may be right, in which case we have commited our lives to an error. It would be wonderful if the reformed epistemologist would extend the same courtesy to us. However, just as we cannot (on principle) refuse to be humble towards him, he cannot (on principle) allow that we might be right. The difference between us is that for the fideist conviction and humility are not incompatible. For the reformed epistemologist, humility is seen as a form of compromising his convictions.

We must accept that we could be wrong. We may be willing to stake our lives on the claim that we are not, but that does not mean that our commitment is a claim to certainty, or at least not a rationally persuasive concept of certainty. Maybe Paul was right. Maybe being a lesbian or a gay man is sinful, wicked, perverted and selfish. We are not saying that this is the case, only that if we are realists about truth we must be humble and admit the possibility of error.

Since we are not the authors of the rules which define a life of faith, we cannot disqualify others from attempting to live the God-relationship. As theists, we find it an incredibly bitter pill to swallow when we are told by the self-proclaimed 'authorities' that we haven't got equal access to faith... unless we undergo a radical disintegration of our persons. The authors of the patriarchal 'norms' which are the rules by which we must *all* attempt to live do not seem to comprehend the frame of reference from which words like 'humility' or 'compromise' derive their meaning for us. For them, humility is a real *choice*, which they have the privilege of nobly making if they so desire. But it makes no sense to ask (or tell) a person for whom the dietary staple is humiliation, to eat humble pie for a change. If your life is compromised by its relative relationship to mine, then compromise isn't a real choice for you. It is too late to ask of you what I've already told you. Is it really a crime to desire anything more for yourself than what it pleases me to give you?

No one has so perfected the art of adding insult to injury as the theocrat. Down the centuries he has excelled at the deceptive craft which makes a virtue out of victimhood. After denigrating the individual by explaining away her self-esteem, he rewards and congratulates the victim's reduced condition, heaping praise and adulation on the 'feminine' virtues of humility and modesty (ie women's uni-lateral subordination to men) and the 'self-discipline' of homosexuals (when they acquiesce in their own oppres-sion by remaining sexually stunted and hence personally crippled). The system works on the same principles as effective advertising; it first takes away the consumer's self-esteem and then offers it back to her at the price of the product. The pecuinary gains of the salesman have their parallel in the social and personal advantages of the moralist. It is a system which fosters *dependence*, for only by means of this one set of values may the individual hope to become whole again. Instead of nurturing people and helping them to achieve their wholeness as individuals, it takes away their independence and proffers a sense of moral vanity in return.

The authentic tradition of prophetic concern for justice and liberation which is so essential a part of Jewish and Chris-tian teaching must concern itself naturally with justice and equality for a minority that has been so viciously perse-cuted down the centuries. The extent and true character of this persecution may never accurately be told, since the authors of history are those who have voices, while the history of homosexuals is one of silence and exclusion. It is no accident that lesbian gay rights activists have made *Silence=Death* their motto.

We feel that it is safe to say, without qualification, that the debt of repentance owed by the churches and Judaism to the homosexual community is in every respect as weighty and serious as that owed by the Christian community to the Jewish community for centuries of persecution, and as owed by the white community to Africans and those of African descent for centuries of enslavement and tyranny.

three

The Perpetuation of Control

One of the fundamental objectives on the agenda of the religious right is the perpetuation of control over people's personal lives. The members of the Ramsey Colloquium state:

> It is important to recognise the linkages among the component parts of the sexual revolution. Permissive abortion, widespread adultery, easy divorce, radical feminism, and the gay and lesbian movement have not by accident appeared at the same historical moment. They have in common a declared desire for liberation from constraint – especially constraints associated with an allegedly oppressive culture and religious tradition.

This statement with its typically *de haut en bas* tone, containing as it does an allegation of moral licence, reveals well the perceptual blind spots of the religious right. It overlooks the fact that on all these issues – abortion, marital morality, the condition of women and homosexuals, intelligent and sincere people hold views that intellectually diverge from those of the religious right. There is a presumption here that the categories employed by the religious right are obviously the correct ones. This begs many rudimentary questions.

Many religious believers (including homosexual ones) deplore the practice of abortion, but religious believers must admit that the conceptual premises which they employ to condemn abortion are not shared by others whose reasons for defending it are just as coherent and morally sensitive as their own. Not everyone subscribes to the concept of the soul; not everyone sees pre-conscious human identity as carrying the same moral weight as conscious and interactive human identity; not everyone agrees that human life is an absolute isolated from other human lives and concerns (compare the Christian tradition on warfare). Adultery and divorce are certainly to be deprecated but to identify a genuine concern over the ambiguities and limitations of the marriage institution is not the same thing as a call to libertarian licence. In the US domestic violence is the single most significant cause of injury to women, more than car accidents, rapes and muggings combined. Fifty per cent of all murdered women in the UK are killed by their husbands, their lovers or a close male relative.

Those who are so sure that traditional family and married life are the right formula for all must prove their case. The family is indeed in crisis for reasons that the religious right have failed to notice. We shall outline these later. The challenge presented by the women's movement must be met in exposing centuries of disempowerment and oppression of women. The gay and lesbian movement is also asking questions about why it has seemed so necessary to hand out such vicious ill treatment to a minority of women and men simply because they are different. It is posing questions that require answers.

Proponents of the traditional agenda have offered no good reason to suppose that there is a distinctively *sexual* morality, in the sense of a specific set of norms which operate in isolation from other spheres of moral consideration. There is no denying that sexual relationships are a delicate type of human relationship; they are especially susceptible to issues of trust, exploitation, infractions involving loyalty to third parties etc, but these are all issues which arise outside of the sexual arena as well. Perhaps we should be looking at what unifies our idea of morality across specific contexts in seeking to answer the questions integral to any single one.

What links this cluster of plaintiffs who allege that culture and religious tradition are oppressive is not a concern for a general throwing over of all restraint but rather the demand for the freedom of people to make fundamental decisions about the management of their own lives. We would not dispute that liberty cannot be absolute, but demand that the standards which are used to impose restraints on liberty do so without destroying the quality of life of any minority. While democracy favours the majority, it is intended to do so without abolishing the basic civil rights of others. Actually it is we who are insisting on a limit to the freedom with which the majority exercises its privileges and powers. When the assumptions generated by the prevailing ideology go unchecked to the extent of interfering with the rights of individuals to privacy and equal protection under law, it cannot persist without justification – given in language which does not merely beg the question by presupposing the superiority of its own beliefs.

Abortion may be a tragedy but so is the domination of women which preys upon the most vulnerable aspect of their sexuality by making it a point of public policy how they are to prioritise between their status as a person and their status as a 'mother'. The atmosphere of blame generated by such policies only disintegrates the status of woman as person and makes her subject to the contents of her uterus, as if this were the more publicly valid aspect of her identity. Similarly a woman's role as 'wife' is thought to supersede her individual personal identity. The overriding concern among pro-choice advocates, feminists, and homosexuals is that people's identities not be relativized according to the straight male's tastes and dictums, which have traditionally been regarded as absolutes.

In the atmosphere which pervades traditional America there is a tacit taboo against being unmarried (especially for females) and even friendly intimacy or displays of affection between males is regarded with an almost paranoid suspicion and contempt. *Everyone* suffers as a result of these sexual stereotypes.

Divorce may be an act of disloyalty, but it may also be the only solution to even worse abuses which the institution of marriage normally conceals within its sanctimonious domain. Women in general do not want to forget all relations with men but they want to stop being defined and controlled by those relations to men and children. Likewise homosexuals want the right, at the very least, to express their sexuality and organise their lives without being molested by others. All of the above movements are marked by a wish to stop the control of persons' lives by third parties, who either address them without understanding their experience or wish to control them for the sake of vested interests of power or identity.

Oppression in its many forms boils down to one thing – the abuse of power. We would even venture to say that all human evil occurs within relationships of inequality which are exploited to the advantage of one party or individual. Destructive power takes many forms: it may be the abuse of physical force or strength, possession of information or secrets which may be used to the detriment of individuals, an unrestrained use of authority granted to bureaucratic or institutional positions, and subtle psychological tools like shame which manipulate people to conspire against themselves in their own oppression.

Men are certainly not the only sex capable of abusing power. However, the bald statistics show that the family has long been a private asylum for the free reign of oppressive abuses which would not be acceptable in the public domain. A 1980 study conducted by Murray Strauss, one of the foremost researchers on violence in the American family, found that male-dominant couples are the type most likely to have experienced a high degree of conflict. In fact, they were almost twice as likely to have high conflict as egalitarian relationships: 39% versus 20% of the egalitarian couples. It does absolutely no good for women to live in democratic countries if their very homes are dictatorships, or plutocracies. To hold up the family as the paragon of moral virtue is to ignore statistical data which indicates that the traditional domicile provides sanctuary from our national ideals of liberty, equality, and justice for all. Not surprisingly, a poll conducted by the *Los Angeles Times* last July found that Clinton's performance rating varied dramatically by gender and marital status: women and single adults were far more satisfied with Clinton than men and those who are married.

four

Special Interests?

Portraying homosexuals as the aggressors has been an effective ploy in garnering support for the religious right's ideals and in creating an atmosphere of paranoia. But this caricature of homosexuals is as laughable as the ant who threatened to trample the elephant underfoot. The most threatening demand made by homosexuals is that they be permitted to openly *exist* without the fear of being assaulted, murdered, or fired from their jobs. The misrepresentation of homosexuals as the ubiquitous 'them' lurking invisibly in our midst and posing a constant threat to our most sacred norms preys upon the very anonymity which it fosters. This anonymity has been thrust upon homosexuals by a heterosexist society, and now that same society denounces these individuals as *subversives*. What choice do homosexuals really have? The only norm that they want to undo is the one which terrorises them into living an ignominious existence. If openly expressing who you are is not considered radical for straights, then how can it be viewed as combative behaviour when applied to homosexuals? When personal honesty becomes a matter of contention because of the normative value judgements which dominate a culture, this ought to be a poor reflection on the state of affairs which promotes such an attitude of oppression, not on the values which are peripheral to it.

Nevertheless, some right wing politicians have had the bald-faced audacity to refer to homosexuals as a 'special interest group', with the implication that they are a group who seek some sort of privilege which the rest of the country does not already enjoy. The unassailable civil liberties which the majority take for granted take on the status of 'special interests' when extended to homosexuals.

What makes them so *special* when applied to gay men and lesbians as opposed to anyone else? This is an obvious double standard. Are homosexuals to be blamed because they take issue with paying dues to a club which refuses to admit them?

Pat Robertson, president of the Christian Coalition, publicised his family values agenda under the slogan, 'Reclaim America'... as if America *ever* belonged to anyone *but* the beneficiaries of the traditions he supports! His attitude bears a frightening resemblance to the posture of Goebbels and Hitler, who assigned prime importance to the so-called 'international Jewish conspiracy' which was the latter's obsession. The following excerpt from Jay W. Baird's study is frighteningly familiar:

> What made the theory even more effective in the hands of the Nazis was that it was never challenged within the Party in any meaningful way, and as a result Nazism did not suffer the dislocations resulting from major theoretical disputes which characterized the Soviet experience.
>
> Hitler's exploitation of anti-Semitism conforms to the the dictum that he offered little ideology that was new; instead he utilized themes which already enjoyed considerable popularity. The Jew had been stereotyped long before the Nazis began to make unashamed use of the prejudice.

Robertson's 1991 book, *The New World Order*, proposed that modern world history has been largely determined by a two-centuries-old conspiracy, with a succession of affluent Jews at the helm. His main source for this theory is a British anti-Semitic writer of the 1920s, Nesta H Webster. In one of her books, Webster discusses the *Protocols of the Elders of Zion* as a possibly authentic document. Baird continues:

> This [widespread contempt for the Jews] was exacerbated by the currency given to one of the more clever

hoaxes of the modern period, the *Protocols of the Elders of Zion*.

So far the theory that homosexuals are a pernicious social threat has not gained full consensus within a political party. However, in the US, Republican House Speaker Newt Gingrich is clearly under pressure from anti-gay extremists and has promised to hold hearings on legislation that would target 'AIDS' prevention programs, promote discrimination against gay youth, and seek to impose federal control over public schools.[15] Similarly, Ollie North, that darling of the Republican right who only narrowly lost his Senatorial bid (despite admitting lying to Congress and being found guilty of serious criminal offences for his role in the Iran-Contra scandal) condemned President Clinton and his 'radical homosexual circles' of 'wanting to sacrifice the world's finest forces on the altar of special interest politics by letting homosexuals into the military'.

The real question behind the 'special interest' rhetoric is what on earth makes the heterosexual male's stance morally neutral? The time has finally come for the patriarch (and his loyal spouse) to justify the privileges which they have enjoyed without restraint in terms which do not boil down to some 'special interest' of their own. Nothing on earth can justify it – which may be why there is suddenly a revived interest in insisting that something in heaven does! This renewed political focus on the divine is no less a *novum* than the social phenomenon which it hopes to undermine.

five

A Time of Change

These movements have emerged at roughly the same time because in North American culture economic and social factors have converged to re-evaluate the old mythologies that held together the traditional, and thereby often religious, justifications of family life and morality. It would seem safe to say that the social fluidity made possible by the impact of two world wars, the greater economic freedom of individuals generally and women in particular, coupled with the advent of reasonably reliable contraception in the 1960s, have converged to shake up the old assumptions.

The wars demonstrated that the sexes could mix together, enjoy each other's company and make choices about sexuality without the need for the traditional protocol and formalities that were formerly considered so essential. They also gave women a taste of freedom and opportunity which they were not in the long run likely to give up. The 1961 film *Splendor in the Grass* (Elia Kazan) stung the conscience of America with its tragic commentary on the social stigma which surrounded sex. The advent of reasonably reliable contraception allowed women to state and pursue sexual satisfaction, which in former times was considered neither desirable nor what women were supposed to want. That particular myth was broken. The greater economic independence of individuals has meant that the family is no longer, in our society at any rate, necessarily a place of security and survival. Individuals have been free therefore to determine their identities and loyalties without automatic reference to the family structure.

This, we believe, has had one important consequence which the religious right has overlooked. As individuals have become freer to form their identities and loyalties without reference to the family a shift has occurred in our culture in the paradigms of relationships. Persons are tending no longer to look towards the family as the ultimate model of security and affection, but rather to friendship for the nurturing and support that families are supposed, traditionally, to give. What this means is that loyalties are *earned* and must therefore be won on their own merits, not on an arbitrary affiliation dictated by happenstance.

This may explain why so many heterosexual couples now choose to live together before marriage or even to dispense with marriage. The traditional family structure is seen as less authentic than the tie of affirming friendship, or else the tie of friendship is considered a better testing ground for loyalty rather than courting, leading inevitably up to marriage, before the risk of marriage is undertaken. This does not necessarily indicate that couples are less committed to each other or stable. It indicates different patterns of loyalty. Of course, it may be admitted that although these developments may be liberating for adults they may be more confusing for children, but even in traditional families children are by no means protected from harm. In fact, according to the findings of a recent American Bar Association report, an estimated 3.3 million to 10 million children witness domestic violence each year in the United States. In nine out of ten cases the mother is the victim, it said. "Family violence is the root cause of virtually every major social problem we face as a nation today", said Sarah Buel, a Boston prosecutor of domestic violence cases. "It is in our homes that children learn that it's OK to use violence to get what you want".

We think that it would not be an exaggeration to say that the so-called 'crisis' in morality is really the result of a tension which exists, now more vociferously than before, between the empirical fact of people's experience and the moral terminology which purports to describe it. If this is the case then it is nothing new, what *is* new is that in the past several decades *real* changes have occured to correct the discrepancy and these changes have taken the reality of people's experience into account so that the meaning of moral terms refers to more than a fairy tale myth. For example, twenty years ago nobody even mentioned 'date rape' because it was assumed, contrary to fact, that the two terms were mutually exclusive. If a young woman (ie a 'girl') even attempted to report a rape in those circumstances, she was automatically a 'bad girl'. Now we use different moral terminology; we call her a 'victim'.

It would seem that right wing Christians want to declare that the 'traditional' ideology is correct and that if anything is wrong it must be that people's lives do not conform to it. The best way to maintain this stance is to encourage a 'reign of silence' or else to keep a constant monologue running so that dissenting voices have no opportunity to interrupt with opposing arguments. What this means is censoring or removing public funding from education, the arts, public libraries and public broadcasting.

six

Ambiguous Places

The lesbian and gay movement is not trying to undermine the institution of heterosexual marriage but it does take strong issue with the pundits of the traditional right who see family as the only normative pattern of cohabitation and who see patterns diverging from it as somehow pernicious to the social fabric. The Ramsey Colloquium states that:

> Marriage and family – husband, wife, and children, joined by public recognition and legal bond – are the most effective institutions for the rearing of children, the directing of sexual passion, and human flourishing in community. Not all marriages and families 'work', but it is unwise to let pathology and failure, rather than a vision of what is normative and ideal, guide us in the development of social policy.

What is so irritating about this statement is not that it makes the assertion that families are the best places to raise children but its steadfast refusal to admit that the family is as ambiguous an institution as the alternatives offered to it.

Families are places where most child abuse takes place, where persons are stunted and illusions fostered, where partners are manipulated and dominated, where evil patterns of behaviour are shrouded in propriety or flatly ignored, where women are beaten and hopes are lost. This is not to say that families are evil places. They are *ambiguous* places where love may be shown and nurtured or warped and destroyed. It cannot be denied that where

Moral Panic

there is evil in family situations that evil is often less easy to tackle precisely because of the official sanctions granted to the 'classic' paradigm of family life. Economic dependency and violence are inextricably linked. Reasearch has consistently shown that economic dependency on men is one of the major reasons why women do not leave violent relationships.[16] The fact is that the ever-precious family values which have had such a prominent political role in villianating the homosexual quest for liberty are not under threat from the *outside* influence of other lifestyles – they are crumbling under the weight of their own failure to provide a safe and humane environment for their own members. Still, proponents of family values are seeking their scapegoats elsewhere. Indeed, a home truth that both the Jewish and Christian religious tradition must acknowledge is that surviving the family atmosphere of traditional Jewish and Christian homes has been in itself a feat that many men and women have had to painfully achieve.

Here we are in an area that is especially relevant to homosexuals. For still probably the majority of homosexual persons, families are places of hurt, denial and often downright rejection. One of the most wounding experiences of being homosexual is that the very people whom one is supposed to most love and trust cannot regard this intimate part of personhood as subordinate to an otherwise comprehensible identity. Instead the person is redefined by reference to the only aspect of their identity which is not comprehensible to others, while dismissing everything that is. Unlike other minorities, gay and lesbian youngsters do not have the comfort of a family or community who share their pariah status. They are completely isolated and have no one with whom to share their fears, frustrations and needs. The forced repression and the danger of abuse to the point of murder account for the fact that gay and lesbian teens are three times more likely to commit suicide than heterosexual teens. Plus, anywhere from thirty to forty percent of homeless and runaway teenagers are homosexual.[17] The most commonly used term of abuse among American grade-school and high school aged kids is 'faggot' or 'fag', and no one bats an eye. If kids threw around racial epithets with the same enthusiasm folks would be up in arms and teachers certainly would not be equally tolerant.

There are, of course, exceptions. There are families where the realisation that a daughter is a lesbian or a son is gay is greeted with understanding, intelligence and unconditional love. This is what ought to occur and what the synagogues and churches ought to be supporting.

seven

Generalities and Myths

The religious right can overlook the realities which confront them by subscribing to the usual generalities and myths about homosexuals that so taint discussion of the subject. What is striking about these generalisations and characterisations is that they talk beyond and over the experience of those whom they are supposed to address. Typical of this is the following passage:

> Advocates of the gay and lesbian movement have the responsibility to set forth publicly their alternative proposals. This must mean more than calling for liberation from established standards. They must clarify for all of us how sexual mores are to be inculcated in the young, who are particularly vulnerable to seduction and solicitation. Public anxiety about homosexuality is pre-eminently a concern about the vulnerability of the young.

This so-called 'concern' for the young is really a concern that they not be given an opportunity, if they are homosexually inclined, to express themselves as such. Yet from the vantage point of those of us who have come out, the role-playing and forced self-abnegation which we experienced in youth are traumas which we do not want other individuals to suffer. There is really no concern for this suffering at all, and even parents whose children are depressed or suicidal because of the rejection would rather 'cure' them than allow their 'concern' to be unconditional.

In the second place, do we really want to *inculcate* our young with sexual mores? Sexuality is integral to the person, not merely to his or her genitalia. Sexuality is a sacred aspect of personal identity, and we don't usually attempt to *inculcate* kids with that. Instead we attempt to set good examples and provide a safe and non-judgmental atmosphere in which it may develop. We have traditionally tried to provide a balance between theoretical teaching and practical skills. In the area of sexuality we must recognise the limitations of theory. The student will no doubt learn much more in practice than from classroom discussions of the biological mechanics of sex. That is due to the profundity of the love relationships through which sexuality is expressed, and to which no mere theory can do justice. This does not reflect a disastrous failure in our teaching methods. It is due to the importance and sublimity of human nature and our ways of growing in relation to other individuals, as opposed to growing in relation to abstract generalisations about 'men', 'women' or 'homosexuals'.

Of course, older homosexuals approach younger homosexuals but then so do older heterosexuals approach younger members of the opposite sex. It is a characteristic of human sexuality that the young carry a certain appeal but it does not define the nature of sexual orientation. What is true, however, is that the lives of many young homosexuals are blighted sometimes for a very long time because they are not supported in doing what their heterosexual counterparts take for granted. If society at large really believes that the presence of an adult homosexual automatically presents a danger to young persons of the same sex then adults of the opposite sex must be banned from single sex school institutions as well – not a very likely scenario nowadays.

Not everything about the homosexual community is good. Among homosexuals there is prostitution, commercial exploitation, ageism, narcissism, selfishness and a tendency to promiscuous self-indulgence. These problems, however, are also endemic among heterosexuals. Having been exiled at the outset from the 'moral' community, it is tempting for homosexuals to just give up all hope of proving their moral integrity. Those that do continue to care have the strength of character and perspicacity to put the good itself ahead of any concerns about whether or not they may enjoy the honour of being identified as guardians of it.

Homosexuals are traditionally more open and candid about sex. Here we agree with the Ramsey Colloquium that the lesbian and gay movement represents a genuine *novum* within the body politic and the religious communities. The frankness with which the gay community lives out and celebrates sexuality poses fundamental questions about the whole tradition of the Judeo-Christian sexual ethic, which has tended to favour the 'low' anthropology found in Paul's epistles. That the church has always had a vested interest in the accompanying soteriology which was part and parcel of the system has never been subject to much critical reflection. At any rate, the breaking of the mythologies about opposite sex relations and family life referred to earlier are lived out by the homosexual community. The gay community is able to live out the truth that sex may form a part of a loving and affirming friendship without interpreting the binding force of that commitment as a matter of public policy. Instead, its parameters are set by ideals of responsible adult behaviour, such as honesty, reciprocity of intention, and mutual fidelity. These are responsibilities which have to be assumed autonomously, or not at all. Human relationships naturally involve risk. It would be foolish to instate laws for the purpose of removing this risk. Love just does not come with insurance policies, and if it did the premiums would be too high!

eight

Alternatives

The members of the Ramsey Colloquium asked the lesbian and gay movement for some clear guidelines on how the young were to be instructed on sexual morality. Sexual morality, like any form of morality, has as one of its principle tenets the sovereignty of individual human persons. This means that people are to be regarded as ends in themselves, not just as vehicles to the self-promotion or fulfilment of others. The traditional 'objective' ethics are very evident, for instance, in the Pope's encyclical *Veritatis Splendor* and the analyses of the ethical right wing in, for example, the pro-life movement. In this tradition the situation is analysed in terms based on 'objective' concepts such as the 'beginning of life', strict definitions of the marriage bond and a certain understanding of 'nature'. Once the situation is analysed in these terms the logical conclusions are drawn. The tradition has the advantage that its conclusions are self-consistent and long-standing. Its disadvantages are that not everyone may agree with the initial premises and concepts and that it tends to ignore the involvement of the participants in the situation. Before anyone can legitimately claim 'objectivity' they must prove that there is more than a grammatical correspondence between their own descriptions of Truth and some reality which exists independently.

The justifications for doing 'objective' subjects are not objective justifications for doing those subjects. The religious right has made considerable advances under the auspices of that strangely tempting fallacy, the 'fat oxen' principle: he who drives fat oxen must himself be fat.

In reflecting on the world that is independent of our experience, we must concentrate not first and foremost on what our beliefs are about, but on whether they honestly represent what they are about. There is a prevalent longing for Truth which tramples over honesty to get at it.

Intuitively most of us would agree that when we speak of morality we mean something more than behaving in a particular way or performing good deeds. In other words, it isn't enough that one merely *acts* as if he were good, one ought really to will the good itself. Kant expressed this notion in his famous dictum: "It is impossible to conceive anything in the world, or even out of it, which can be taken as good without limitation, save only a good will".[19] To define certain outward acts as moral or immoral may simply be an impossibility, since we can never ascertain whether a good act corresponds to a good will or to a mental state of desiring the good itself above all other interests.

In the antitheses of Matthew 5.21-48 Jesus shifts the emphasis from behaviour to intention, or will: 'You have heard that it was said to men of old, 'You shall not kill; and whoever kills shall be liable to judgement'. But I say to you that everyone who is angry with his brother shall be liable to judgement', and 'You have heard that it was said that 'You shall not commit adultery'. But I say to you that everyone who looks at a woman lustfully has already committed adultery with her in his heart'. The responsibility is not to *act* as if one were good (to do so presupposes some definite public idea of the good which one can mimic) but to genuinely do good in a spirit of good will. The importance of this concept of Spirit is reiterated by Jesus in Mark 3.28-30 and John 14.17. The concept of Spirit found in Paul's epistles is the antithesis of this. Paul thinks of Spirit as a motivating force which animates people when they are doing particular acts which he has already defined as good, and which is absent from anyone who disobeys or deviates from these prescriptions. Paul's idea of Spirit is rather superstitious and undermines free will... and the personal responsibility which accompanies it.

If Fred helps a blind man across a busy intersection his behaviour would be described by any ordinary observer as 'good'. However, although some actions are *prima facie* 'good', there are cases where they are not genuinely motivated by the good itself but are conditional. For example, if Fred is aware that Ginger (his very attractive female co-worker) happens to be observing his kind gesture, this factor may be the real motive behind his good deed. The religious enthusiast, likewise, is acting from prudence and not from duty or goodwill if his kindness towards others is motivated by an awareness of God (envisaged as a Big Brother figure who will reward or punish him according to his final score). God is not Santa Claus! He may see you when you're sleeping and know when you're awake and whether you've been bad or good .... but *be good for goodness sake*. The problem with many Christians is that they have reduced the good to a means to selfish ends, such as salvation. This, again, may be traced to Paul and his immanentist eschatology, which proved to be wrong.

It might be added that the real reason why America got good moral vibes from *Forrest Gump* was not that he represented typical Protestant values. On the contrary! Gump represents a form of moral innocence which cannot be reduced to egocentric motives such as salvation or the Pauline idea of 'righteousing oneself'. Gump's innocence bears a natural relation to his own corporeal experience, through which he has developed an instinct for sympathy and a sensitivity to the experience of others. Gump is not on some perverse mission to transcend his humanity in order to score atonement points with the deity. He is a figure of moral innocence because he doesn't have the sort of shrewd, calculating mind that could conceive of a good act as a means to a self-centered end. For Forrest Gump virtue is its own reward... a notion which has become quite alien to our modern minds. The style of life which his character represents is a sharp rejoinder to those who preach Biblical moral dogma, for it proves that they haven't even comprehended the first book! The moral wisdom and discernment which some claim is their exclusive privilege is the forbidden fruit. Innocence, on the other hand, is a humble acceptance of the human condition, through which we can always find common ground with other human beings. The film's main protagonist, Forrest Gump, is disadvantaged from birth and in this respect he is symbolic of the heroic underdog. Like the downtrodden types he represents, Gump is innocent of his condition. Fate or 'destiny' is responsible for his I.Q., but what makes that an 'evil' is the social stigma, the taboo which accompanies being different (or as some prefer to say, 'dysfunctional'). Gump is a throwback to an era when people were not sophisticated enough to calculate the profits of every single act and when love was not equated with sexual power and control. He runs for the sake of it, not to score touchdowns. He keeps promises because that is what a promise means. He puts his life at risk to save a friend because that's what friendship is. For Gump it is the principle of the thing and the principle is not modified with reference to some end external to it which he just happens to value. There are loads of honest and morally sensitive Americans who saw that film and loved it – they just couldn't figure out why. The critics trashed the film because they were so eager to sniff out a rat and expose it in their usual cynical way. This time sophisticated liberals shot themselves in the foot, and perhaps it is because we *all* have become desensitized to Forrest's way of thinking, on both sides of the fence. Forrest Gump couldn't be further removed from the religious right's politicized version of 'Christianity', which markets the idea that conventional morals are a means to self-preservation, either in Heaven or on earth.

The new ethic may have its disadvantages as does the more traditional ethic, but we would suggest that it is one that is becoming more dominant in our society. It is the failure of the religious right to understand it that results in the fact that its spokesmen so often talk over the heads of those whom they address.

nine

Back to Basics?

In the winter of 1993/4 Britian's Prime Minister John Major attempted to import the brand of neo-Conservatism which had been so successful in the US by coining the slogan 'Back to Basics'. It conjured up the wholesome 'family values' which have been broadly represented as the antithesis of feminism and homosexual rights. While it was rather ambiguous what the real emphasis was on at the Conservative Party Conference, it seemed that single parents bore the brunt of the criticism. This rebounded on the parliamentary Conservative Party when it was revealed that many of its members were fathering illegitimate children of their own or were otherwise involved in forms of tawdry self-contradiction. The succession of scandals had the immediate impact of taking the momentum out of the Back to Basics agenda, but its proponents have formed a Christian pressure group which aims at marrying biblical exegesis and principles with public policy. At the vanguard is MP David Altman, co-founder of the Movement for Christian Democracy and a spokesman for Parliamentary campaigns to change the abortion law. The movement is roughly based on a set of six 'Guiding Principles' which are outlined in its founding declaration. They are: *Social Justice* (as founded in the character of God and given by divine law); *Respect for Life* (human beings are created in the image of God); *Reconciliation* (The Kingdom of God is heralded by a community in which we are all to be reconciled in Jesus Christ); *Active Compassion* (The God of justice is the God of love; we are called to active loving service of others); *Wise Stewardship* (All economic activity involves our responsibility before God for the world entrusted to us); and *Empowerment* (Authority is given from God for the common good; those who have power are to be accountable).

The problem, as we see it, is that the proponents of theocracy want to unite two irreconcilable sources of authority. On the one hand, they acknowledge that their stance is an ideological world view which involves *choosing* to regard the Bible as the infallible source of Truth on moral issues, and on the other hand they want to institute this world view as absolute law. So while admitting that fundamentalist Christianity is one of many possible alternatives, they will not concede any possible internal fallibility in doctrine. The equation is something like this: we have a theory, which in practice we refuse to treat as though it were merely a theory. What this means is that if their dream of creating a 'Christian society' were ever to come true, it would necessarily have to work on authoritarian principles. What most often happens in such contexts is that the 'human fallibility' defence is dragged in on convenient occasions (as when the moral authorities are caught in hypocrisy) but is thoroughly denied in matters which involve the interests of those who are most affected by its moral pronouncements. There is no recourse for those who stand to lose as a result of this assymetrical application of 'divine' law.

Despite the wording of the declaration's sixth principle (above), the heirarchy is constructed so that those at the top are least accountable...except to 'God', a Being whose so-called 'character' is given content exclusively by the *men* it serves. The biblical basis for policy is especially damning for women and children, since all of the books of the cannon were written by men in an age which gave women only slightly more social status than the animals, and have been translated and interpreted by men ever since. The following remarks by C S Lewis hint at what Back to Basics seeks to restore:

On the other hand, [a Christian society] is always insisting on obedience – obedience (and outward marks of respect) from all of us to properly appointed magistrates, from children to parents, and (I'm afraid this is going to be very unpopular) from wives to husbands. Thirdly, it is to be a cheerful society: full of singing and rejoicing, and regarding worry and anxiety as wrong.[20]

In other words, not only will women and children be subjugated, but they will accept their condition cheerfully. And if they experience 'anxiety' as a result, then it is *they* who are to blame. Lewis is quick to admit that very few would like this sort of society in its entirety. Most people would like parts of it but not the whole. Lewis suggests that it is in the nature of Christianity that people take what they like and reject the rest, so that often two people's definition of Christianity can be quite different. The implication is that if your definition of 'Christianity' differs from the New Testament one, then it is because you're selective in what you choose to obey. But of course, since males selected the New Testament in the first place, and since Paul exercized a great deal of selection in his interpretations of the then sacrosanct Hebrew Bible, Lewis is all too right that it is *in the nature of Christianity* that 'people' take what they like and reject the rest – that is what 'Christianity' *is*, a view on reality which reflects what certain males like. Alison Webster's conclusion is most accurate:

> What has happened, I think, is that we now recognize that moral relativism is all we ever had, but that some people had the power to portray their subjective judgements as objective face, as 'the way things should be' or as 'God's will'.[21]

The affirmation that rulers of a Christian society must be 'confined' to a Christian framework is all very well, but if the framework itself cannot evolve or be seriously questioned, then the scope for interpretation can never involve a challenge to the presuppositions which engendered the original blueprint. This leaves far too little room for the learning and discovery which constitute the evolution of human understanding. For example, until the discovery of the female ovum in the 1820s, the basic assumption of female inferiority was underpinned by the false belief that males provided the biological seed for creation and women were simply a convenient place to plant it. Hence, the claim that women were equal to men qua progenitors would have involved a factual error. We now know that in fact our understanding of the correspondence between our terms and empirical fact was flawed, and as a result our knowledge has evolved. This is precisely the type of evolution which our opponents hope to block with respect to the discovery of the gay gene.

David Porter, in his pithy summary, *Back to Basics: the Anatomy of a Slogan*, draws an analogy between the Christian code of ethics and Plato's vision in the *Republic:* "that once having defined moral laws, they should never be changed, for in their existence and continuity the health of the popular soul lay".[22] But the circularity of this conception of the so-called 'popular soul' is evident in the following quotation, which Porter uses to bolster his argument for a conjunction of the ideal (envisioned as 'God') and the practical application of it in law:

> The Guardians whose tenure and powers make them tolerably *independent of popular pressures*, should themselves obey the laws in all things, and interpret them when necessary in the spirit in which they were framed.[23]

The spirit in which biblical laws were framed (ie defined) took little account of the 'health of the popular soul', unless the 'popular soul' refers to an ancient all-male Greco-Roman soul which has nothing of value for the health of modern day women, much less the women of their own era!

Of course it may, and probably will, be argued that in taking the equal rights of women for granted *we* are merely exercizing a cultural prejudice for which there is no good basis. It is at this juncture that our Christian faith diverges most radically from that of our opponents. Their criteria for judging the Truth of moral propositions is a version of human reason (ie 'natural law'). In *Christianity and Social Order* William Temple (1881-1944) gave a prototype for the 'Basics' which many of our modern-day theocrats would like to return to:

It is wholesome to go back to the old conception of Natural Law because it holds together two aspects of truth ... the ideal and the practical. ... The conception of Natural Law will help us to frame the *right* or ideal relation between the various activities of men and of the men engaged in them. [my emphasis][24]

Archbishop Temple and our more modern critics of the 'dislocation of the structure of life' are intent to rebuke any criteria of progress which interprets the structure of life in genuinely egalitarian terms. As Porter is adept to point out, Temple argued that there had been an inversion of the natural order, 'things had become ends in themselves, not ends to the life of *man*'. [my emphasis] If by 'things' the Archbishop meant women, then he is certainly right. We have already shown that the meanings of words can evolve due to the fact that they are relative to the human ends and purposes which they serve. But Temple and company seem to think that *certain* definitions should never evolve significantly, since their meaning is related to a 'higher' truth. Yet this higher truth is in fact reductionist for it involves assent to the credal doctrines of the Christian church, which maintains that an anthology of 66 books was the vehicle God chose to reveal himself, through the inspiration of the Holy Spirit, to humanity. There are pre-suppositions here which are indefensible on the basis of rational argument, such as the notion that there exists a metaphysical Being, God, who is concerned about the affairs of human beings. While *we* are comfortable to exist as Christians on the periphery of the rational world and to humbly submit to the limitations of a faith-based world view, our opponents seem to want to do the opposite, that is, to re-order the rational world according to the beliefs which they think best explain reality.

The choice to view the bible as the most relevant criterion for the establishment of moral laws in society is itself a human judgement, and this judgement is by no means rational, except in the most naive sense. If God is just conscience, then there is no need to multiply meta-physical entities. Let's set the God talk aside and have a conscientious dispute. If these were the terms of our argument we would no doubt lose, because *our* ultimate conviction rests on faith in God – and since God is something independent of our conscience we must be humble. We are not the best judges of what is true or right – God is – and we trust God to vindicate ourselves even though we cannot. Humility towards others is, *ex hypothesi*, our mandate.

ten

What's in a 'Nature'?

There is no proof that homosexuality is not genetic. Many recent studies suggest that there is a gay gene. The testimony of many sincere lesbians and gay men that they 'always felt this way' may end up not to be a coincidence. Homosexuals may just be another manifestation of the incredible diversity of God's creation. Our opponents know that, with the Human Genome Project currently underway, conclusive proof of this theory may be forthcoming in the not too distant future. The members of the Ramsey Colloquium expressly state that:

> To those who say that this disordered behaviour is so much at the core of their being that the person cannot be (and should not be) distinguished from the behaviour, we can only respond that *we earnestly hope* they are wrong. [my emphasis]

What is this but an admission by homophobes that they are reluctant to accept evidence which would prove that their long-standing value judgement against homosexuals is based on a misunderstanding of human nature? One would have thought that the genetic evidence (if discovered) would settle once and for all the 'natural law' argument against homosexual normality. But not so, say our opponents. Their argument is that, while some scientific evidence suggests a genetic predisposition for homosexual orientation, the case is not significantly different from evidence of predispositions towards other traits, for example, alcoholism or violence. The analogy is unconvincing and tendentious. The 'dispositions' which they claim are comparable to homosexuality are ones which are known to be self-destructive or socially destructive. Besides the fact

Moral Panic

50

that society does not pass moral judgements on self-destructive behaviour like smoking, there are value judgements being made on homosexuality to the effect that consenting sexual relationships between adults of the same sex are socially destructive. The Ramsey Colloquium's statement makes this quite clear:

> The social norms by which sexual behaviour is inculcated and *controlled* are of urgent importance for families and for the society as a whole. [my emphasis]

and

> Another legitimate reason for public concern is the harm done to the social order when policies are advanced that would increase the incidence of the gay lifestyle...

In a country where a rape occurs every six minutes, the hypothetical threat to society posed by homosexuality is a red herring. It betrays a mis-evaluation (or false description) of the social norms which dictate sexual behaviour. There is a very fine line separating our public understanding of what is 'natural' from what is *normative*. Not one conservative Christian figurehead has made a national issue out of the rape epidemic. Instead it is tacitly assumed that sexually agressive and violent behaviour is 'natural' in males, implying that they are genetically predisposed to such behaviour. Yet has this popular belief given rise to fear and concern among 'Christians' who purport to be concerned about 'society as a whole'? On the contrary, men have acquiesced in this particular construction of their sexuality, usually in order to escape moral responsibility for their actions.[25] But we suggest that men are not intrinsically sexually incontinent. Rather, rape has become normative (ie routinized) in our society. The slide from the 'normative' to the 'natural' is an illicit attempt to redefine fact according to value. In the case of homosexuality, then, what is ab-'normal' (ie not normative, or routinized) is illicitly stigmatized as un-'natural'. This selective method of description betrays the inconsistency which typifies the Ramsey Colloquium's document. It's members admit that they cannot settle the dispute about the roots of homosexual orientation (genetic or environmental), and then go on to say that no analogy can be drawn between the homosexual movement and the civil rights movement, since 'differences of race are in accord with – not contrary to – our nature..'. The implication is that *even if* homosexuality is found to be genetic, it cannot be 'natural'. This is a radical presumption which has no basis in fact, and so hopes to establish it in grammar.

What is going on here is that we are moving from a definition of 'nature' to the conclusion that there is actually just such a nature. 'A bachelor is an unmarried man' does not, for example, say anything about any particular existing bachelor. It tells you what the word 'bachelor' means in English, and what it applies to. To ascertain its truth you need not observe any particular bachelor; all you need to do is to understand the concept. On the other hand, if I say 'All bachelors are unfulfilled' the predicate is not contained in the subject. You would have to actually observe and interview all the bachelors there are to ascertain whether the statement is true or false. In the argument against the possibility of a homosexual nature, the illicit move is from 'a nature is...' to 'there is a nature...'. Again, it is far from certain that the conceptual premises employed here correspond to any real facts. The concept is purely analytic. The question that begs to be asked is what makes these definitions true, other than fiat, habit or persuasion?

'It is *impossible* that a unicorn does not have a horn' may be true, but this does not prove that *there are* unicorns. Once you have understood what a unicorn is, then you will see that a unicorn cannot be hornless. Likewise, once you have understood what we mean by 'nature', you cannot fail to see that a nature cannot be homosexual. But all this tells us nothing about the reality of or existence of a particular human nature, it only tells us about the IDEA of a nature.

Homosexual men and women do not usually purport to be merely living 'alternative lifestyles'. This phrase is a contrivance of heterosexist politicians and theologians who do not respect that our sexuality is an integral part of our humanity – not a 'disposition' or a faddish habit. No one is more down on scientific explanations or the modern technological treatment of human affairs than the religious believer. She feels that her faith is threatened by the more 'simple' or 'rational' explanations of natural phenomena which tend to dominate secular culture and which make her appear 'backwards' or superstitious. Yet oddly, when it comes to sex, no one is quicker to embrace a strictly anatomical explanation of sexuality than the religious believer. Sexuality, if it is to be affirmed as a mode of expressing love, must fit the monolithic biological model: penile penetration of a vagina. This reductivist view of sexuality dehumanizes the nature of the union – it is less a union of two people than of two sexes, or worse, two organs! The enormous emphasis on reproduction (especially in Roman Catholicism) portrays sexuality as though it were *primarily* 'functional' ... a means to an end. This also dehumanizes heterosexual love, by making the human relationship subordinate to the biological one.

The notion that it is OK to be homosexual just so long as you don't act on the 'evil' impulse trivializes the homosexual relationship, reducing it to the level of a lusty vice ("It's OK to hanker after a cigarette, just don't smoke one"). The presumptions made by our accusors about what our relationships consist of, namely *selfish desire*, are not accurate. This is no surprise, given the usual double-standard. It is doubtful whether they would describe their own inclinations to form meaningful relationships with partners of their choice as mere selfishness; most would agree that love relationships are *necessary* to our human growth and flourishing. It is their own presumptions about us which our opponents attack most vehemently.

Interestingly enough, the very argument that Martin Luther used to defend the practice of marriage for Protestant ministers as opposed to celibacy is also an airtight defence for homosexual partnerships. According to Luther, marriage and other secular enterprizes are not bad and sinful in themselves, but *we* are bad and sinful. Sin is a disease with which we are all infected from birth (according to the doctrine of original sin). Luther maintained that the fall had spoiled even the things in the world which we regard as good. It is our attitude to God and to our own desires which spoils the good institution of matrimony. It is entirely wrong, in Luther's view, to try to escape sinful things by celibacy or the monastic life. One cannot avoid the sins of the world by foresaking the world. Asceticism and self-denial cannot exalt a person above the 'world' and may be a form of extreme selfishness. It will do no good for a heterosexual Protestant to try to achieve righteousness by denying *his* sinful desires or instincts; only belief in Jesus Christ's salvific power can justify him. There is no need to change his lifestyle in addition to believing. Given this view of marriage, it is difficult to see how modern day Protestants can recommend to homosexuals that they abstain from their sinful 'desires', unless they are shamelessly deploying a blatant double-standard.

eleven

An Unnecessary Problem?

Whatever may be the traditions held in the Judeo-Christian ethic about homosexuality, we would suggest that those who maintain that homosexual acts are intrinsically wrong are under an obligation to show why the suffering that this causes so many individuals is necessary. Certainly homosexuals will get it wrong, will exploit others and make foolish decisions. This is a problem among heterosexuals as well. Why do human beings have a passion for inventing unnecessary difficulties over such matters as sexual orientation, race, nationality or creed? The inclusion of the other matters may seem unfair but what the modern world asks of religious believers who condemn homosexuality is to prove to them that what they are exercising is not just a cultural prejudice.

The story about the destruction of Sodom and Gomorrah had no association with 'sodomy' in Jewish tradition until what Christians call the inter-testamental period and then only appears definitely in the writings of Philo of Alexandria in the first century CE. The Christian tradition on sodomy is a borrowing from the elaboration's of Judaism. There is even speculation that the centurion's servant cured by Jesus in the Gospel of Saint Luke could, as his batman, also have been his lover – a common situation in the Roman army of the period. This is evidenced by the use in the Greek original of the word *pais* for the servant boy (boy, child, servant or *boyfriend* in the homosexual sense) rather than the more usual *doulos* (servant or slave).

Even if this exegesis cannot be insisted on, Jesus probably had a fair idea of the full gamut of human sexuality. Certain members of the religious right might do well to join Jesus in his overriding concern for the love commandment, by putting themselves in the shoes of the oppressed just long enough to reflect on their condition.

Notes

1 'The Homosexual Movement: A Response by the Ramsey Colloquium' in *The Month*, ed. John McDade, July 1994, p.260.

2 House of Bishops, *Human Sexuality*, para. 4.8, p.34.

3 *Understanding Veritatis Splendor*, ed. John Wilkins, London, SPCK, 1994, 'A Summons to Reality' Oliver O'Donovan, p.45.

4 Jay W Baird *The Mythical World of Nazi War Propaganda 1939–1945*, University of Minnesota Press, 1974, p. 4

5 *The New Republic*, March 13, 1995, p.23.

6 *Multiculturalism and the Politics of Recognition*, Charles Taylor with commentry by Amy Gutmann, ed. et al., Princeton, New Jersey: Princeton University Press, 1992.

7 See Peter C Vardy, *The Puzzle of God*, Harper Collins, 1995. Vardy is an expert on the realism/anti-realism distinction and this book outlines the issues very clearly.

8 A J Ayer, *The Problem of Knowledge,* Penguin, 1956, p. 25

9 Michael Peterson, 'Faith and Reason: How Are They Related' in *Reason and Religious Belief*, Oxford University Press, 1991, p. 39.

10 Peterson, pp. 37-38.

11 Soren A Kierkegaard, *Concluding Unscientific Postscript*, trans. David F Swenson and Walter Lowrie, Princeton, NJ: Princeton University Press, 1941, p.182.

12 For a clear and concise discussion of this view see Peter C Vardy's *The Puzzle of God*, Harper Collins, 1995.

13 Martin E Marty, 'What is Fundamentalism? Theological Perspectives', in Hans Kung & Jurgen Moltmann eds., *Fundamentalism as an Ecumenical Challenge*, Concilium 1992/3, London SCM 1992, p.6.

14 R S Woolhouse, *The Empiricists*, Oxford University Press, 1988, p.15.

15 *The New York Native*, Feb.6, 1995.

16 Julie Francis, 'Women take action' in *Women Against Fundamentalism Journal*, no.5, 1994, Vol. 1, p.63.

17 Women's Action Coalition, *WAC Stats: The Facts About Women* (New York: BRAT An Arts Organization, 1992) pp. 19 and 21.

18 Ramsey p. 264

19 Immanuel Kant, *Foundations of the Metaphysics of Morals*, in 'The Theory of Ethics', trans by T K Abbott, sixth edition, London: Longmans, Green and co. Ltd. 1963, p. 9.

20 C S Lewis, *Christian Behaviour*, Bles, 1943, p.18.

21 Alison Webster, *Found Wanting*, Cassell Plc., 1995, p.195.

22 David Porter, *Back to Basics: the Anatomy of a Slogan*, OM Publishing, 1994, pp.78-87, quoted from p.87.

23 Plato, trs. Trevor J Saunders, *The Laws*, Penguin, 1970, Saunders's introduction, p.33.

24 William Temple, *Christianity and the Social Order*, Penguin, 1942, p.59.

25 Alison Webster, *Found Wanting: Women, Christianity and Sexuality*, Cassell Plc., 1995, p.38.